T0001565

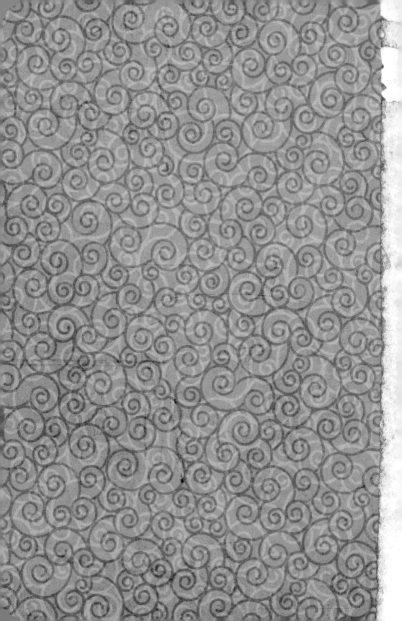

PRAYERS & PROMISES
FOR
Daily
Strength

CONTENTS

Introduction

We all experience difficult seasons in life that
sap us of our energy. Loss, pain, anxiety, sickness, or
frustration can lead to discouragement and sometimes a
feeling of exhaustion.

Prayers & Promises for Daily Strength is a topically
organized collection that guides you through themes of
assurance, inspiration, endurance, rest, purpose, and
more. Encouraging Scriptures, heartfelt prayers, and
prompting questions give you an opportunity to think
more deeply about the joy and truth found in God's Word.

By staying connected to God, and believing in his
promises, you can be renewed and re-energized, drawing
on his strength to live a fulfilling, blessed life. Take a
moment to breathe in the calming peace of his presence.
He cares for you, and he will always be with you.

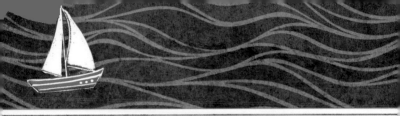

Abandonment

"The LORD himself goes before you and will be with you;
he will never leave you nor forsake you."

DEUTERONOMY 31:8 NIV

The Lord loves it when he sees us walking in his justice.
He will never desert his devoted lovers;
They will be kept forever in his faithful care.

PSALM 37:28 TPT

God has said,
"I will never fail you. I will never abandon you."
So we can say with confidence,
"The LORD is my helper,
so I will have no fear."

HEBREWS 13:5-6 NLT

"I will not abandon you as orphans—
I will come to you."

JOHN 14:18 NLT

God, you say over and over in your Word that you will not leave me. Give me eyes to see you when I feel alone. Let my heart know your nearness when I cry out to you. You never turn away from those who need you, and oh, how I need you in this moment! I will cling to the truth that your ever-present help is at hand, especially when I've reached the end of my rope. Today, may the comfort of your presence melt away every fear and lead me into love.

Do you truly believe that God will never leave you?

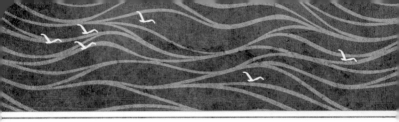

Ability

"My grace is sufficient for you, for my power is made perfect in weakness." Therefore I will boast all the more gladly of my weaknesses, so that the power of Christ may rest upon me.

2 Corinthians 12:9 esv

After you have suffered for a little while, the God of all grace, who called you to His eternal glory in Christ, will Himself perfect, confirm, strengthen, and establish you.

1 Peter 5:10 nasb

Take a new grip with your tired hands and strengthen your weak knees. Mark out a straight path for your feet so that those who are weak and lame will not fall but become strong.

Hebrews 12:12-13 nlt

Sometimes, Lord, I question your call on my life. I deeply desire to follow you and do great things in your name, but I don't trust my own humanity. Thank you for the numerous examples in the Bible of times you chose to use weak men and women to carry out your mission. Thank you for the times in my life when you've used me despite my shortcomings. May they serve as a reminder that true strength is only found in you. Thank you for having grace with my inabilities and granting me the ability to proceed with what you have called me to do.

Do you believe that God can make you able to do what he asks?

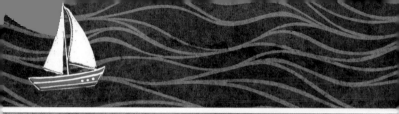

Acceptance

"The Father gives me the people who are mine. Every one of them will come to me, and I will always accept them."

JOHN 6:37 NCV

The LORD does not see as man sees;
for man looks at the outward appearance,
but the LORD looks at the heart.

1 SAMUEL 16:7 NKJV

If God is for us,
who can be against us?

ROMANS 8:31 ESV

In love he chose us before he laid the foundation of
the universe! Because of his great love, he ordained
us, so that we would be seen as holy in his eyes with an
unstained innocence.

EPHESIANS 1:4 TPT

Father, I have struggled with feeling less than, being left out, and feeling alone. Your Word tells me that is a lie, for I have been chosen, specifically created, and given purpose by the God of the universe. You have promised to never leave me. Your Holy Spirit is my indwelling companion. No matter how I look or feel, your affection never changes for me. Help me see others as beautifully as you see me, never judgmentally but always with acceptance. Thank you for the glorious truth that I am created in your image.

How does God's acceptance of you help you to be more accepting of others?

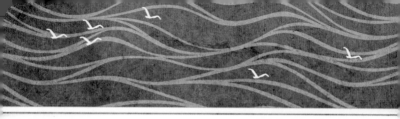

Anxiety

Lord, you are my shield,

My wonderful God who gives me courage.

I can lie down and go to sleep, and I will wake up again,

Because the Lord gives me strength.

Thousands of troops may surround me,

but I am not afraid.

PSALM 3:3, 5-6 NCV

"Don't let your hearts be troubled.

Trust in God, and trust also in me."

JOHN 14:1 NLT

Give all your worries to him,

because he cares about you.

1 PETER 5:7 NCV

I was desperate for you to help me in my struggles,

and you did!

PSALM 120:1 TPT

Jesus, I am fraught with worry, fearful from imagining all that could go wrong. The daily news hangs like a dark cloud over my head. When I turn to your Word, I am enlightened, seeing clearly that you have a plan that cannot be thwarted. You alone open doors that no one can shut and close doors no one can open. Only you are all powerful. You reign victorious forevermore. Help me to be consistently in your Word and on my knees in prayer. Increase my faith for I know you alone are my help and my salvation.

What steps can you take to be less anxious and more trusting?

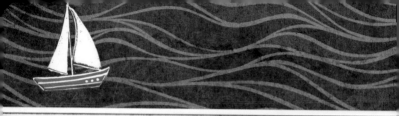

Assurance

To him who is able to do immeasurably more than all we
ask or imagine, according to his power that is at work
within us, to him be glory…for ever and ever! Amen.

EPHESIANS 3:20–21 NIV

All of God's promises have been fulfilled in Christ
with a resounding "Yes!"

2 CORINTHIANS 1:20 NLT

I go to bed and sleep in peace,
because, LORD, only you keep me safe.

PSALM 4:8 NCV

These things I have written to you who believe in the
name of the Son of God, that you may know that you have
eternal life, and that you may continue to believe in the
name of the Son of God.

1 JOHN 5:13 NKJV

Lord, there is nothing on this earth that can enter my life that has not passed through your hands. You created me for a purpose and desire to do more in me than I can ever ask or imagine. Even if I devised the grandest scenario, you have far greater things in store. At times I feel my faith is not big enough. Help me in my unbelief. I want to be a warrior for Christ, a world changer for the gospel. With you I know all things are possible!

How does believing God's promises cause you to feel reassured?

Authenticity

"Remember this: If you have a lofty opinion of yourself
and seek to be honored, you will be humbled. But if you
have a modest opinion of yourself and choose to humble
yourself, you will be honored."

MATTHEW 23:12 TPT

What should be our proper response to God's marvelous
mercies? I encourage you to surrender yourselves to God
to be his sacred, living sacrifices. And live in holiness,
experiencing all that delights his heart. For this becomes
your genuine expression of worship. Stop imitating the
ideals and opinions of the culture around you, but be
inwardly transformed by the Holy Spirit through a total
reformation of how you think. This will empower you to
discern God's will as you live a beautiful life, satisfying
and perfect in his eyes.

ROMANS 12:1—2 TPT

Father, knowing that you see to the core of my heart is at times wonderful and at others frightening. I desire that you make my heart your home, yet sometimes I feel I have invited you into a dirty house. My sin ruins the appearance of a soul that desires so desperately to please you but falls short. When I confess it is as if my living quarters are deeply cleansed, for in your mercy, you pardon my iniquity. I sincerely desire to worship you and humbly offer my life as a living sacrifice to your goodness and salvation.

How do you see yourself?
How do you think God sees you?

Beauty

Your beauty should come from within you—the beauty of a gentle and quiet spirit that will never be destroyed and is very precious to God.

1 PETER 3:4 NCV

Hold on to wisdom and good sense.
Don't let them out of your sight.
They will give you life
and beauty like a necklace around your neck.
Then you will go your way in safety,
and you will not get hurt.

PROVERBS 3:21-23 NCV

She is clothed with strength and dignity;
she can laugh at the days to come.

PROVERBS 31:25 NIV

God, I love the way you view beauty. How wonderful it would be if the world saw as you do, looking at the inner person, not the outer. You desire our character to be the fruit of the Spirit and our attire to be your armor. So opposite from the covers we see on magazines, you look past the appearance and go straight to the heart. You made me exactly as you wanted me to be, and I know you rejoice and sing over me. I praise you for I am fearfully and wonderfully made!

How does beauty look different to you after reading these verses?

Belief

"For God so loved the world that he gave his one and only Son, that whoever believes in him shall not perish but have eternal life. For God did not send his Son into the world to condemn the world, but to save the world through him. Whoever believes in him is not condemned."

JOHN 3:16, 18 NIV

To all who did accept him and believe in him
he gave the right to become children of God.

JOHN 1:12 NCV

Believe on the Lord Jesus Christ,
and you will be saved.

ACTS 16:31 NKJV

"Blessed are those who have not seen
and yet have believed."

JOHN 20:29 ESV

Father, I confess that at times a slight doubt creeps in.
In those times when I see such evil in the world, I wonder
where you are and why you allow it? Then I remember it
is our choice to sin, wreaking havoc within ourselves and
spilling it onto others. You provided a way of escape by the
means of salvation. If we will accept your Son's sacrifice and
confess our sin, we will be saved for now and eternity. Thank
you for your loving plan that provides forgiveness from my
transgressions and life everlasting.

How can you strengthen your belief in God?

Boldness

He proclaimed the kingdom of God
and taught about the Lord Jesus Christ—
with all boldness and without hindrance!

Acts 28:31 niv

The wicked flee though no one pursues,
but the righteous are as bold as a lion.

Proverbs 28:1 niv

On the day I called you, you answered me.
You made me strong and brave.

Psalm 138:3 ncv

Let us come boldly to the throne of our gracious God.
There we will receive his mercy, and we will find grace
to help us when we need it most.

Hebrews 4:16 nlt

Lord, why do I ask you so intently to give me the opportunity to give witness to my faith and then shrink back. My heart pounds and mind races as if my life were in danger. I know it is pride that prevents me from sharing. I fear what man will say. Forgive me and give me strength and power through your Holy Spirit to share the great news of the gospel. Help me to be ready with an answer for any who ask. I pray that nothing will stop me from speaking the truth of your magnificent salvation.

Why is it sometimes hard to be bold?

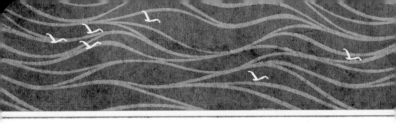

Change

Look! I tell you this secret:
We will not all sleep in death,
but we will all be changed.

1 Corinthians 15:51 NCV

He will take our weak mortal bodies and change them
into glorious bodies like his own, using the same power
with which he will bring everything under his control.

Philippians 3:21 NLT

Jesus Christ is the same yesterday and today and forever.

Hebrews 13:8 NIV

I will not be afraid, because the Lord is with me.
People can't do anything to me.

Psalm 118:6 NCV

Dear Lord, the thought of being freed from a body that is prone to illness and pain is amazing, yet the uncertainty of when this change is coming can be unsettling. There is that element of the unknown. I admit that I wish I had a heads-up about your return, but your Word says you are coming at an hour that no one knows. I do rejoice in the fact that when we see you, we will be like you. Realizing my frail being will be transformed into an eternal and indestructible body like yours is incredible. Help me long for that day with faith and hopeful expectation!

How do you handle change?

Comfort

"God's dwelling place is now among the people,
and he will dwell with them.... 'He will wipe every
tear from their eyes. There will be no more death'
or mourning or crying or pain."

Revelation 21:3–4 niv

May our Lord Jesus Christ himself and God our Father,
who loved us and by his grace gave us eternal comfort
and a wonderful hope, comfort you and strengthen you.

2 Thessalonians 2:16–17 nlt

Unless the Lord had helped me,
I would soon have settled in the silence of the grave.
I cried out, "I am slipping!"
but your unfailing love, O Lord, supported me.
When doubts filled my mind,
your comfort gave me renewed hope and cheer.

Psalm 94:17–19 nlt

Father, just knowing that I am never out of your sight, always within your reach and under your wings of protection, brings indescribable peace. Jesus said on this earth I would suffer trials and tribulation but to take heart, for he has overcome the world. I know how it all ends and the result is victorious, eternal life. Thank you that while I am living this side of heaven, I am surrounded by your constant presence, comforting grace, and never-ending love. You alone are my hope and salvation.

Do you feel the comforting presence of God today?

Compassion

When I am with those who are weak, I share their
weakness, for I want to bring the weak to Christ.
Yes, I try to find common ground with everyone,
doing everything I can to save some.

1 CORINTHIANS 9:22 NLT

Have mercy on me, O God,
according to your unfailing love;
according to your great compassion
blot out my transgressions.

PSALM 51:1 NIV

Praise be to the God and Father of our Lord Jesus Christ,
the Father of compassion and the God of all comfort.

2 CORINTHIANS 1:3 NIV

The LORD hears his people when they call to him for help.
He rescues them from all their troubles.

PSALM 34:17 NLT

Lord, how wonderful it is to be understood, listened to, and helped in times of need. When my heart is breaking and someone willingly enters my emotions with me, comforting and giving wise counsel, it is healing balm. I am so thankful that you, my heavenly Abba, will always graciously invite me into your presence to bear my soul and receive your compassion. Help me to show your loving care and speak words of healing to others. You alone have the answer to all that life brings, and you alone are worthy of praise.

How can you be a more compassionate person?

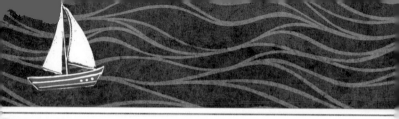

Composure

God is the one who saves me;
I will trust him and not be afraid.

ISAIAH 12:2 NCV

You will sleep like a baby, safe and sound—
your rest will be sweet and secure.
You will not be subject to terror, for it will not terrify you.
Nor will the disrespectful be able to push you aside,
because God is your confidence in times of crisis,
keeping your heart at rest in every situation.

PROVERBS 3:24-26 TPT

If people's thinking is controlled by the sinful self, there
is death. But if their thinking is controlled by the Spirit,
there is life and peace.

ROMANS 8:6 NCV

Jesus, this is too hard, and I feel paralyzed by all that is falling apart around me. Sometimes I want you just to rewind time and let this all play out differently. If I try in my flesh to fix this difficulty, I will most assuredly get it wrong and could even make it worse. Please take this from me and if not, carry me through it. Precious Redeemer, I trust in you. I know you are my refuge. As in times past when it was darkest before the dawn, I will remember your morning mercies. I know you will deliver me as I wait and watch with unwavering assurance.

How can you remain steady when it feels like your world is crumbling around you?

Confidence

I can do everything through Christ,
who gives me strength.

PHILIPPIANS 4:13 NLT

Be my rock of refuge,
to which I can always go;
give the command to save me,
for you are my rock and my fortress....
For you have been my hope, Sovereign LORD,
my confidence since my youth.

PSALM 71:3, 5 NIV

Perfect, absolute peace surrounds those
whose imaginations are consumed with you;
they confidently trust in you.

ISAIAH 26:3 TPT

Lord Jesus, all things are possible with you. There is no event, no problem, no foe that you cannot conquer with the utmost skill, wisdom, and excellence. Even if the mountains crumble around me, I have nothing to fear for you will protect me. My strength may be miniscule, but with your power I can tackle the strongest offender. My confidence is buoyed by my belief in your unlimited, supernatural ability. I trust in you, rejoicing that I can face anything that comes my way for you will defend me, my rock, and my fortress!

How do you find your confidence?

Consolation

You, LORD, are a shield around me,
My glory, and the One who lifts my head.

PSALM 3:3 NASB

Blessed be the LORD,
Because He has heard the sound of my pleading.
The LORD is my strength and my shield;
My heart trusts in Him, and I am helped;
Therefore my heart triumphs,
And with my song I shall thank Him.

PSALM 28:6-7 NASB

He did rescue us from mortal danger, and he will rescue
us again. We have placed our confidence in him, and he
will continue to rescue us.

2 CORINTHIANS 1:10 NLT

Father, as my head hangs in distress and my heart breaks in a million pieces, I can feel you drawing me to you. You are my helper. You are my healer and I hand you my heart to hold and repair. I know you will make good out of evil. As you lift my head and call me to keep my eyes focused on you, I find hope. Though it feels like this could kill me, I know and believe in you, the source of life. I will rest in your power to pull me through to victory, restoring what was lost with your best plan for me. Your comfort revives me.

How do you feel you have been consoled by God in your moments of grief?

Contentment

It is a good thing to receive wealth from God and the good health to enjoy it. To enjoy your work and accept your lot in life—this is indeed a gift from God. God keeps such people so busy enjoying life that they take no time to brood over the past.

ECCLESIASTES 5:19-20 NLT

I know what it is to be in need, and I know what it is to have plenty. I have learned the secret of being content in any and every situation, whether well fed or hungry, whether living in plenty or in want. I can do all this through him who gives me strength.

PHILIPPIANS 4:12-13 NIV

Those that the LORD has rescued will return. They will enter Zion with singing; everlasting joy will crown their heads. Gladness and joy will overtake them, and sorrow and sighing will flee away.

ISAIAH 35:10 NIV

Lord, I confess that I look at what others have, comparing and coveting. I wonder why their life is so easy and favored. I feel less valued than those who appear to have it all. I realize this is a lie from the pit. What more could I want, for I have you Jesus? I have been given everything I could ever desire in my salvation, forgiveness, and assurance of eternity with you. I have your presence with me always, and I belong to a heavenly family. I praise you today, for I truly have been given your very best and rejoice over your magnificent gifts to me.

How can you choose to be content with your life as it is right now?

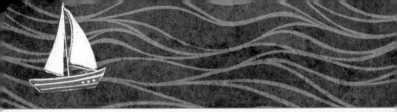

Courage

Be strong in the Lord and in his mighty power. Put on the
full armor of God, so that you can take your stand against
the devil's schemes.

EPHESIANS 6:10-11 NIV

Be alert. Continue strong in the faith. Have courage, and
be strong. Do everything in love.

1 CORINTHIANS 16:13-14 NCV

Even though I walk through the darkest valley,
I will fear no evil, for you are with me;
your rod and your staff, they comfort me.

PSALM 23:4 NIV

"This is my command—be strong and courageous! Do
not be afraid or discouraged. For the LORD your God is
with you wherever you go."

JOSHUA 1:9 NLT

Lord, your Word says when I am at my weakest, you are most able. Today, I have no strength, no energy, and no words for what I am facing. I need your power and I am believing with all my heart what your Scripture says is true. I need your bravery to face the tense adversity I must step into. I need your almighty wisdom and courage to walk this out in a way that brings restoration. Please glorify yourself through this situation. Keep me from doing anything in my own flesh and show yourself strong on my behalf.

When was the last time you asked God for courage?

Delight

When your words came, I ate them;
they were my joy and my heart's delight,
for I bear your name,
Lord God Almighty.

Jeremiah 15:16 niv

"My God, I want to do what you want.
Your teachings are in my heart."

Psalm 40:8 ncv

Your laws are my treasure;
they are my heart's delight.

Psalm 119:111 nlt

"Let your light shine before others, that they may see
your good deeds and glorify your Father in heaven."

Matthew 5:16 niv

Abba, I wish I could see myself as you see me. I find every issue, every flaw, and I magnify it. I see myself as the black sheep not the beloved child of God. I want so desperately to alter this. I ask for wisdom and revelation so that I may know your Son better because I believe when you look at me, you see him. I have been transformed by my faith in Christ and to you, I am most beautiful. You know me intimately; you desire and sing over me. I receive your truth about me, that I am favored and adored by my Lord.

How hard is it for you to fathom God's incredible delight in you?

Deliverance

I waited patiently for the Lord;
he turned to me and heard my cry.
He lifted me out of the slimy pit,
out of the mud and mire;
he set my feet on a rock
and gave me a firm place to stand.
He put a new song in my mouth,
a hymn of praise to our God.
Many will see and fear the Lord;
and put their trust in him.

PSALM 40:1–3 NIV

Humble yourselves in the sight of the Lord,
and He will lift you up.

JAMES 4:10 NKJV

Father, I know that you hold the entire world in your hands and that without your approval, the sun wouldn't rise. When I awake in the morning, alive and breathing, I know it is only because you have ordained it. Forgive me for fearing what hasn't even happened and may never transpire. And, if the worst occurs, you will be there to hold me, comfort me, and deliver me. Help me to live with my whole heart what I know to be true in your Scripture. You have saved me and will bring me faithfully into your presence, protected and secure through the blood of Christ.

What fears do you need to be delivered from?

Depression

Why am I so sad? Why am I so upset?
I should put my hope in God
and keep praising him.

PSALM 42:11 NCV

You, O LORD, are a shield about me,
my glory, and the lifter of my head.

PSALM 3:3 ESV

He has delivered us from the power of darkness and
conveyed us into the kingdom of the Son of His love.

COLOSSIANS 1:13 NKJV

"I am Yahweh, your mighty God!
I grip your right hand and won't let you go!
I whisper to you:
'Don't be afraid; I am here to help you!'"

ISAIAH 41:13 TPT

Jesus, why do I feel as if there is a massive dark cloud overshadowing me? I know intellectually that you are my healer and comfort, yet I find it impossible to rejoice. Take hold of my heart and lift my head to see my salvation. I understand that my hope is in you, but I need your Spirit's power to access it. Deliver me from this despair and transport me to a place of complete confidence in you. You are my reward. I will praise you until my soul is lifted and my joy is restored.

Can you sense God's comfort and joy in the middle of your sadness?

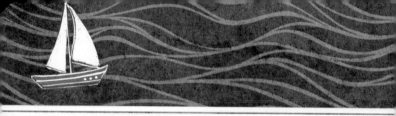

Encouragement

The LORD your God is with you;
the mighty One will save you.
He will rejoice over you. You will rest in his love;
he will sing and be joyful about you.

ZEPHANIAH 3:17 NCV

Encourage one another daily,
as long as it is called "Today."

HEBREWS 3:13 NIV

Kind words are like honey—
sweet to the soul and healthy for the body.

PROVERBS 16:24 NLT

Be joyful. Grow to maturity. Encourage each other.
Live in harmony and peace.
Then the God of love and peace will be with you.

2 CORINTHIANS 13:11 NLT

Father, I know how much it benefits my heart when someone encourages me. It is so effortless, yet the most kind, to give a good word to another. It not only brightens the day of the receiver but lifts the spirit of the one who speaks it. Help me look for opportunities to bless others by reminding them of who they are in Christ. I pray that my conversations will be characterized by compassion and lovingkindness. May I listen so closely for what your Holy Spirit would like to say to another through my voice. Help me obey and speak joyfully to those around me.

How can you encourage someone today?

Eternity

We are citizens of heaven, where the Lord Jesus Christ
lives. And we are eagerly waiting for him to return
as our Savior.

PHILIPPIANS 3:20 NLT

"If I go and prepare a place for you, I will come back and
take you to be with me that you also may be where I am."

JOHN 14:3 NIV

It will happen in an instant—in the twinkling of his eye.
For when the last trumpet is sounded, the dead will come
back to life. We will be indestructible and we will be
transformed.

1 CORINTHIANS 15:52 TPT

Surely your goodness and love will be with me all my life,
and I will live in the house of the LORD forever.

PSALM 23:6 NCV

Jesus, you created a dwelling in heaven with me in mind. How glorious to think of what my place in heaven is like! I know I can't begin to imagine the stunning beauty of what your love has built for me. The best part though, is that I will be with you forever, able to see you and give you praise. Tears of joy fill my eyes as I consider how I will be able to look right into yours! I am grateful beyond comprehension of all that I have been given and will one day experience in your presence.

Can you view eternity with a hopeful, happy heart, fully trusting in a good God?

Faith

Through Christ you have come to trust in God. And you
have placed your faith and hope in God because he raised
Christ from the dead and gave him great glory.

1 PETER 1:21 NLT

"I promise you, if you have faith inside of you no bigger
than the size of a small mustard seed, you can say to this
mountain, 'Move away from here and go over there,' and
you will see it move. There is nothing you couldn't do!"

MATTHEW 17:20 TPT

The important thing is faith—
the kind of faith that works through love.

GALATIANS 5:6 NCV

Faith is confidence in what we hope for
and assurance about what we do not see.

HEBREWS 11:1 NIV

Father, your Word is resplendent with promises that I only
need to believe, and then anything is possible. As the father
of the possessed boy in Mark 9:24 cried out, so do I; "I believe,
help me in my unbelief." When I think of the things you have
prepared for me, things I can't even imagine, I feel inspired
and hopeful. As I learn to trust that I will experience and see
these things, my confidence soars. Please give me the kind of
faith that never wavers and knows without a doubt that you
can work miracles on my behalf.

What helps increase your faith?

Faithfulness

Your mercy, LORD, extends to the heavens,
Your faithfulness reaches to the skies.

PSALM 36:5 NASB

The Lord is faithful, who will establish you
and guard you from the evil one.

2 THESSALONIANS 3:3 NKJV

LORD, you are my God;
I will exalt you and praise your name,
for in perfect faithfulness
you have done wonderful things,
things planned long ago.

ISAIAH 25:1 NIV

The word of the LORD is upright,
and all his work is done in faithfulness.

PSALM 33:4 ESV

Precious Savior, as I look back over the course of my life, I am amazed and humbled at your faithfulness. Forgive me for all the times that I spent hours, days, in worry of what may come instead of remembering your goodness and trusting in you. I have come to the eleventh hour but never the twelfth without you answering in your wisdom and providing what you knew was best for me. When your answer has been no, I've felt your loving presence saying to wait and see, for you always turn ashes into beauty. Thank you that no matter what, I can depend on my loving heavenly Father.

How have you seen the faithfulness of God played out in your life?

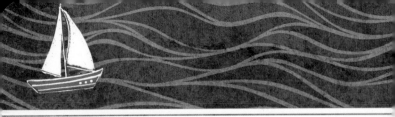

Fear

God will never give you the spirit of fear, but the Holy
Spirit who gives you might power, love, and self-control.

2 Timothy 1:7 TPT

The Lord is my light and my salvation—
whom shall I fear?
The Lord is the stronghold of my life—
of whom shall I be afraid?

Psalm 27:1 NIV

We can say with confidence, "The Lord is my helper,
so I will have no fear. What can mere people do to me?"

Hebrews 13:6 NLT

When I am afraid, I will trust you.
I praise God for his word.
I trust God, so I am not afraid.
What can human beings do to me?

Psalm 56:3-4 NCV

Dear Abba, this world is so frightening at times. There is so much evil, and I find myself getting suspicious of who I can believe or trust. I fear for my loved one's future and then feel guilty because I know you are in control. When I get anxious, help me to run to you so you can restore my confidence in your almighty power. I pray I will stand unafraid because I know who I have believed in, and you are completely able. I lay my cares at the foot of your cross; you alone are my salvation.

What fears can you give to God right now?

Forgiveness

He is so rich in kindness and grace that he purchased our
freedom with the blood of his Son and forgave our sins.

EPHESIANS 1:7 NLT

As far as the east is from the west,
So far has He removed our wrongdoings from us.

PSALM 103:12 NASB

If we confess our sins, He is faithful and just to forgive us
our sins and to cleanse us from all unrighteousness.

1 JOHN 1:9 NKJV

"Her sins—and they are many—
have been forgiven, so she has shown me much love.
But a person who is forgiven little shows only little love."

LUKE 7:47 NLT

Lord, I am hurt, angry and don't understand why I have been mistreated by someone I trusted. I was blindsided by an unfair act and confess that I have wallowed in the offense. I am having a hard time wanting to see this person again let alone forgive them. Please soften my heart toward them and help me make this right by extending forgiveness and acceptance even if not asked for it. Help me remember all you have forgiven me of and move me to be gracious in offering mercy and love.

Is there someone who needs your forgiveness today?

Freedom

The Lord is the Spirit,
and where the Spirit of the Lord is,
there is freedom.

2 CORINTHIANS 3:17 NIV

Beloved ones, God has called us to live a life of freedom.
But don't view this wonderful freedom as an excuse to set
up a base of operations in the natural realm. Constantly
love each other and be committed to serve one another.

GALATIANS 5:13 TPT

"If the Son sets you free, you are truly free."

JOHN 8:36 NLT

We have freedom now, because Christ made us free.
So stand strong. Do not change and go back into the
slavery of the law.

GALATIANS 5:1 NCV

56

Father, I rejoice in your truth. I have been set free from the law of sin and death. I praise you, Jesus, that because of your sacrifice in taking my place on the cross, I am exempt from the punishment I deserved. May I never take this lightly or excuse ill actions because I can simply confess. Give me a heart that desires to live a righteous and holy life before you. Please fill me with your Spirit and help me to refuse temptation and the prison that sin can chain me in. I am free in Christ, and I never want to live any other way!

How does it feel to be free from your sin?

Friendship

A friend loves you all the time,
and a brother helps in time of trouble.

Proverbs 17:17 NCV

There are "friends" who destroy each other,
but a real friend sticks closer than a brother.

Proverbs 18:24 NLT

"Greater love has no one than this: to lay down one's
life for one's friends. You are my friends if you do what
I command…. Instead, I have called you friends, for
everything that I learned from my Father I have made
known to you."

John 15:13–15 NIV

"In everything, do to others
what you would have them to do to you."

Matthew 7:12 NIV

Father, I am thankful that you created us for relationships. The fellowship of believers is a blessing, and much encouragement is found in supporting one another in Christ. I want to thank you for your body, the church, and how you gifted each member to work together in complementing one another to fulfill your purpose. I praise you today for each wonderful sister and brother in Christ you have placed in my life to walk with me and to serve alongside. I am grateful for friendships that are bonded in you.

What friends spur you on in your relationship with God?

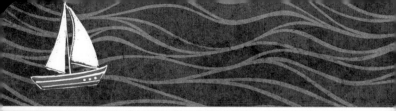

Goodness

Everything God created is good, and nothing is to be
rejected if it is received with thanksgiving.

1 Timothy 4:4 NIV

Taste and see that the Lord is good.
Oh, the joys of those who take refuge in him!

Psalm 34:8 NLT

I remain confident of this:
I will see the goodness of the Lord
in the land of the living.

Psalm 27:13 NIV

They will tell about the amazing things you do,
and I will tell how great you are.
They will remember your great goodness
and will sing about your fairness.

Psalm 145:6-7 NCV

Dear Father, I get defensive when people question your goodness. They cast blame on you for the deeds that men do. I have experienced your goodness in times of plenty and times of need. The end game for you is always loving victory that extends to your creation. Even when a situation doesn't look good, the result is always your best for us. Your ways and thoughts are not as ours, and we must trust your wisdom in all of life's outcomes. I will testify of your lovingkindness in the things you have wrought. You are holy and righteous in all you do.

Where do you see the goodness of God in your life?

Grace

From his fullness we have all received,
grace upon grace.

God gives us even more grace,
as the Scripture says, "God is against the proud,
but he gives grace to the humble."

JAMES 4:6 NCV

Sin is no longer your master, for you no longer live
under the requirements of the law. Instead, you live
under the freedom of God's grace.

ROMANS 6:14 NLT

Christ gave each one of us the special gift of grace,
showing how generous he is.

EPHESIANS 4:7 NCV

Lord, I am monumentally thankful that when I confess, in your grace you forgive and forget. I can move forward in my relationship with you, unencumbered by fear of rejection or the weight of my failings. As I humble myself, your kindness and mercy toward me flows in abundance. I praise you, for you are the definition of generosity and benevolence. I have seen it repeatedly, for there are no limits to your blessings. I have hope and a future because of your goodness. I place my life in your hands knowing that only there am I safe and secure.

What does God's grace look like in your life?

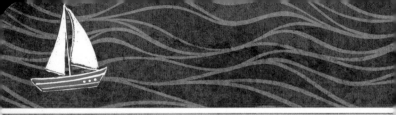

Gratitude

I have not stopped giving thanks for you,
remembering you in my prayers.

EPHESIANS 1:16 NIV

Giving thanks is a sacrifice that truly honors me.
If you keep to my path,
I will reveal to you the salvation of God.

PSALM 50:23 NLT

Rejoice always, pray continually,
give thanks in all circumstances;
for this is God's will for you in Christ Jesus.

1 THESSALONIANS 5:16–18 NIV

Enter his gates with thanksgiving
and his courts with praise;
give thanks to him and praise his name.

PSALM 100:4 NIV

Lord, I am ecstatic with joy over my position in Christ. Your Word tells me that I am chosen and because of the sacrifice of Jesus, I am holy and blameless in your sight. I am a daughter of the king, adopted and sealed by your Holy Spirit. You have redeemed me and lavished me with wisdom and understanding. Your care for me extends to knowing the number of hairs on my head. Your compassion carries my tears in a bottle. Thank you that your plan for me was designed out of your purpose and great love. I pray I can glorify you today out of gratitude for your goodness to me.

What can you thank God for right now?

Grief

Those who sow in tears shall reap with shouts of joy.

PSALM 126:5 ESV

Let your steadfast love become my comfort
according to your promise to your servant.

PSALM 119:76 NRSV

"Come to me, all you who are weary and burdened, and I
will give you rest. Take my yoke upon you and learn from
me, for I am gentle and humble in heart, and you will
find rest for your souls."

MATTHEW 11:28-29 NIV

Every valley shall be raised up,
every mountain and hill made low;
the rough ground shall become level,
the rugged places a plain.

ISAIAH 40:4 NIV

Jesus, I doubt that I can produce any more tears. I have soaked my bed with my anguish. Your Word promises that the energy I have exerted in my sorrow will be turned into shouts of joy. Please, in your great mercy, move on my behalf and get me to the other side where I can find my smile again. Even now, I am beginning to feel your comfort and reassurance that you have already provided the answer to my problem. I have only to stand still and watch you fight for me. Thank you for the rest you are releasing into my soul; I stand in faith for my conquering comforter.

Do you ask God for help when you need his comfort?

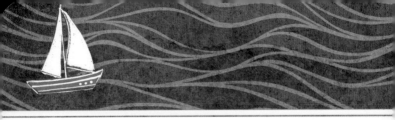

Guidance

Guide me in your truth and teach me,
for you are God my Savior,
and my hope is in you all day long.

PSALM 25:5 NIV

I praise the LORD because he advises me.
Even at night, I feel his leading.
I keep the LORD before me always.
Because he is close by my side,
I will not be hurt.

PSALM 16:7-8

We can make our plans,
but the LORD determines our steps.

PROVERBS 16:9 NLT

Those who are led by the Spirit of God
are children of God.

ROMANS 8:14 NIV

Father, your Word says that if I ask for wisdom and believe, you will grant it to me. I am requesting this gift and placing my faith in your promise. I can't navigate my current situation or any aspect of my life without your revelation. I am so thankful you are with me, guiding and keeping my feet solidly on your path. Lead me in your ways of righteousness and allow my actions to bring you glory. You are my only hope. Show me how to follow you, walking with you in lock step so I remain on the straight and narrow road.

Is there anything God can help guide you in today?

Guilt

If we confess our sins, he is faithful and just and
will forgive us our sins and purify us from all
unrighteousness.

1 John 1:9 NIV

Because the Sovereign Lord helps me,
I will not be disgraced,
Therefore have I set my face like flint,
and I know I will not be put to shame.

Isaiah 50:7 NIV

Those who go to him for help are happy,
and they are never disgraced.

Psalm 34:5 NCV

I have not achieved it, but I focus on this one thing:
Forgetting the past and looking forward to what
lies ahead.

Philippians 3:13 NLT

Lord, I know when I confess my sin you are faithful and just to forgive my sin. You even cast them into the depths of the ocean where they cease to exist. I confess I have gone diving, digging them up to ruminate over. I pause any effort to participate in praise and worship because I am ashamed. Help me remember that these sins of mine have been paid for, resulting in my freedom from guilt. Lead me to share my testimony of your faithfulness so others can find salvation and deliverance. Help me bring you glory by sharing my witness so others can find your gracious forgiveness.

Why doesn't God want you to feel guilt and shame?

Health

The world and its desires pass away,
but whoever does the will of God lives forever.

1 JOHN 2:17 NIV

Do not be wise in your own eyes;
Fear the LORD and shun evil.
This will bring health to your body
and nourishment to your bones.

PROVERBS 3:7-8 NIV

I will never forget your commandments,
for by them you give me life.

PSALM 119:93 NLT

A happy heart is like good medicine,
but a broken spirit drains your strength.

PROVERBS 17:22 NCV

Jesus, you told us that we would face suffering in this world, so what I'm experiencing now should come as no surprise. I believe that if I put my trust in you as my great physician you will provide the recovery that I require. I know that as I pray, I must surrender to your will—your idea of my healing in this life. I know I can speak of your goodness regardless of what your plan for me looks like. Today, though, I ask for relief, for restoration of my health. I want the opportunity while on this earth to tell others of your great compassion and power.

What healing are you believing God for right now?

Hope

The LORD is good to those whose hope is in him,
to the one who seeks him.

LAMENTATIONS 3:25 NIV

This hope is not a disappointing fantasy, because we can
now experience the endless love of God cascading into
our hearts through the Holy Spirit who lives in us!

ROMANS 5:5 TPT

God has given both his promise and his oath. These two
things are unchangeable because it is impossible for God
to lie. Therefore, we who have fled to him for refuge can
have great confidence as we hold to the hope that lies
before us. This hope is a strong and trustworthy anchor
for our souls. It leads us through the curtain into God's
inner sanctuary.

HEBREWS 6:18-19 NLT

Jesus, when it comes to appealing to you in prayer, there is nothing that I cannot bring before you. I have confidence because of who you are, that I will be heard and the answer will be on its way before I even speak. After all, you know my needs before I ever voice them. My hope is complete and free from doubt because I know your character that is never changing. I will believe in the good things you have for me with hopeful expectations. You are love, you are faithful, and you are the one I can trust in every situation.

Knowing that God always hears you, what can you be hopeful for?

Identity

See how very much our Father loves us, for he calls us
his children, and that is what we are! But the people who
belong to this world don't recognize that we are God's
children because they don't know him. Dear friends, we
are already God's children, but he has not yet shown us
what we will be like when Christ appears. But we do know
that we will be like him, for we will see him as he really is.

1 JOHN 3:1-2 NLT

Do everything without grumbling or arguing, so that
you may become blameless and pure, "children of God
without fault in a warped and crooked generation." Then
you will shine among them like stars in the sky as you
hold firmly to the word of life.

PHILIPPIANS 2:14-16 NIV

Oh Lord, when I hold myself up against the front cover of a popular magazine, I want to hide. I don't and never will compare to the model who is pictured. They are perfect and I am far from it. But you see me differently. You see your child who was made in your exquisite image. You see your purpose and plan that you ordained before I was even born. You see someone you cared enough about to sacrifice your only Son for. My identity is in you. I praise you that I am dearly loved and live as a transformed being in you.

Who do you think God really sees when he looks at you?

Inspiration

The precepts of the LORD are right,
giving joy to the heart.
The commands of the LORD are radiant,
giving light to the eyes.

PSALM 19:8 NIV

Your laws are my treasure;
they are my heart's delight.

PSALM 119:111 NLT

God has transmitted his very substance into every
Scripture, for it is God-breathed. It will empower you by
its instruction and correction, giving you the strength to
take the right direction and lead you deeper into the path
of godliness.

2 TIMOTHY 3:16 TPT

Almighty God, what an incredible privilege it is to have your living Word! It has the power to leap off the page and infuse itself into my life. What a joy it is to have a road map to life. It speaks to me, warning me of the consequences of sin. It offers forgiveness and salvation through the cross of Jesus Christ. It shows me the beauty and splendor of my eternal home complete with streets of gold and jeweled gates. I joyfully delight in the wisdom of your Word. Thank you for your truth that enlightens my path and strengthens my soul, helping me live a holy life before you.

How do you find inspiration?

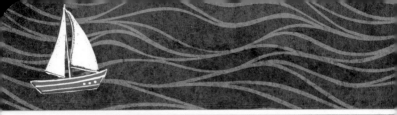

Joy

May the God of hope fill you with all joy and peace as you
trust in him, so that you may overflow with hope by the
power of the Holy Spirit.

ROMANS 15:13 NIV

"Don't be sad, because the joy of the LORD
will make you strong."

NEHEMIAH 8:10 NCV

The LORD is my strength and shield.
I trust him with all my heart.
He helps me, and my heart is filled with joy.
I burst out in songs of thanksgiving.

PSALM 28:7 NLT

Be cheerful with joyous celebration
in every season of life. Let your joy overflow!

PHILIPPIANS 4:4 TPT

Father, yesterday was hard but today is another story. In the depths of the day before you gave me strength and hope for the next. Waiting on you, Lord, is accompanied by a feeling of eager expectation. I can laugh at the future for I know you have already been there preparing it for me, and it is good. I can live with an exuberant heart because my God in his wisdom has all the answers. I have absolute peace because you, Lord, hold the future. You have overcome, and the result is the promise of eternity in your heavenly kingdom.

What is one truly joyful moment you've had recently?

Kindness

Be kind to each other, tenderhearted, forgiving one
another, just as God through Christ has forgiven you.

Ephesians 4:32 nlt

Kind people do themselves a favor,
but cruel people bring trouble on themselves.

Proverbs 11:17 ncv

Do the riches of his extraordinary kindness make you
take him for granted and despise him? Haven't you
experienced how kind and understanding he has been to
you? Don't mistake his tolerance for acceptance. Do you
realize that all the wealth of his extravagant kindness is
meant to melt your heart and lead you into repentance?

Romans 2:4 tpt

God, it is hard to show kindness to someone who has been unkind to me. Initially it shocks me that such a situation has taken place. I feel numb. Then I remember how kind you have been to me every time I have offended you with my sin. Mine is a far greater transgression than any that could be perpetrated against me. Please give me your Spirit of love and mercy toward others. Take the hurt and turn it into grace that results in joy for both sides who have found freedom to forgive and forget.

How can you extend kindness to those around you today?

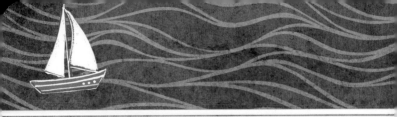

Life

All praise to God, the Father of our Lord Jesus Christ.
It is by his great mercy that we have been born again,
because God raised Jesus Christ from the dead. Now we
live with great expectation.

1 PETER 1:3 NLT

That faith and that knowledge come from the hope for life
forever, which God promised to us before time began.

TITUS 1:2 NCV

"I am the way and the truth and the life.
No one comes to the Father except through me."

JOHN 14:6 NIV

The Word gave life to everything that was created,
and his life brought light to everyone.

JOHN 1:4 NLT

Father, I love your mercies that are new every morning. When I take my first breath of the day, I acknowledge that it is only because of your goodness. Then as I look to your Word, I read of the life eternal that was gifted to me by believing in the name of Jesus Christ, and I am filled with exuberant joy. I am so grateful for your salvation that brings freedom from sin and the assurance of a future in your heavenly kingdom. Thank you for the abundant life you have given me on this earth and the future day when I will live with you forever.

What is your favorite part of life?

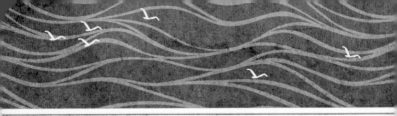

Loneliness

"Teach them to obey everything that I have taught you,
and I will be with you always,
even until the end of this age."

MATTHEW 28:20 NCV

The LORD is near to all who call on him,
yes, to all who call on him in truth.

PSALM 145:18 NLT

Even if my father and mother abandon me,
the LORD will hold me close.

PSALM 27:10 NLT

"Be strong and courageous. Do not be afraid or terrified
because of them, for the LORD your God goes with you;
he will never leave you nor forsake you."

DEUTERONOMY 31:6 NIV

Lord, there are times when it seems like everyone has retreated just when I need them the most. You specifically made us for relationships and when that is lacking it is heart shattering. Please send me a companion that shares the same love I have for you. I know you are the friend that sticks closer than a brother, but right now, I just need some friendships to do life with here on earth. I trust that you will answer my prayer and, in the meantime, continue to hold me close and comfort me with your presence.

When you feel lonely, can you turn to God and ask him to surround you with his presence?

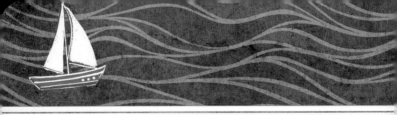

Loss

Those who sow in tears shall reap with shouts of joy.

PSALM 126:5 ESV

Let your steadfast love become my comfort
according to your promise to your servant.

PSALM 119:76 NRSV

LORD, have mercy, because I am in misery.
My eyes are weak from so much crying,
and my whole being is tired from grief.
In my distress, I said,
"God cannot see me!"
But you heard my prayer
when I cried out to you for help.

PSALM 31:9, 22 NCV

Lord, there is nothing on this earth that can assist me. My only help comes from you. You are the source of wisdom and comfort. You alone have the answer to all of life's difficulties. I am weary and have no ability to handle this. I am thankful that this is a good thing, for your Word says when I am at my lowest, you are the lifter of my head. Help me look to the day when I will rejoice, for I will speak of how you delivered me. Even now, I have hope knowing that you will never leave me or forsake me.

Do you ask God for help when you need his comfort?

Love

Three things will last forever—
faith, hope, and love—
and the greatest of these is love.

1 CORINTHIANS 13:13 NLT

You, LORD, are forgiving and good,
abounding in love to all who call to you.

PSALM 86:5 NIV

Where God's love is, there is no fear, because God's
perfect love drives out fear. It is punishment that makes
a person fear, so love is not made perfect in the person
who fears.

1 JOHN 4:18 NCV

Fill us with your love every morning.
Then we will sing and rejoice all our lives.

PSALM 90:14 NCV

Father, I am so thankful for your Word which says to love one another as you have loved us. When I try to comprehend the vastness of your love for me and how I can replicate that to others, I know I cannot do it on my own. You also say if I don't love others then I can't love you, which breaks my heart. Please help me. Will you love others through me? Please give me your heart for all your creation. Your extravagant love for me compels me to love others; I want to please you in all I do. Create your heart in me.

How does the love of God in your life help you to love others?

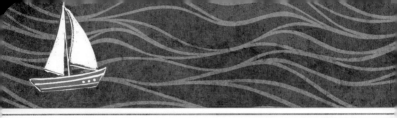

Patience

Warn those who are lazy.
Encourage those who are timid.
Take tender care of those who are weak.
Be patient with everyone.

1 THESSALONIANS 5:14 NLT

Be like those who through faith and patience
will receive what God has promised.

HEBREWS 6:12 NCV

Be completely humble and gentle;
be patient, bearing with one another in love.

EPHESIANS 4:2 NIV

Whoever is patient has great understanding,
but one who is quick-tempered displays folly.

PROVERBS 14:29 NIV

Lord, I confess that I can feel my blood approaching its boiling point. Certain life situations push my buttons, and I seem to lose all ability to steady my emotions. How can I be holy when I am exhibiting such lack of control? I desperately need you. Please give me patience, understanding, and compassion through the power of your Holy Spirit. I pray you will prick my conscience when I start to sin and help me redirect my actions so they please you. Help me to be a holy representative of Jesus in every way possible.

How can you show more patience in your life?

Peace

"I have told you these things,
so that in me you may have peace.
In this world you will have trouble.
But take heart! I have overcome the world."

JOHN 16:33 NIV

The LORD gives his people strength.
The LORD blesses them with peace.

PSALM 29:11 NLT

May the Lord of peace himself give you peace at all times
and in every way. The Lord be with all of you.

2 THESSALONIANS 3:16 NIV

"I am leaving you with a gift—peace of mind and heart.
And the peace I give is a gift the world cannot give.
So don't be troubled or afraid."

JOHN 14:27 NLT

Lord God, Jehovah Shalom, your name is peace. In this world, it seems like peace is a totally foreign concept. Every time I open my phone, the news that flashes is nothing but negative and full of fear. You warned us this life would bring trouble, yet you shared that you have already achieved victory. I know I can rest in the fact that I am safe and secure because my Savior is almighty, all-powerful, and has already conquered sin and the grave. I will not be afraid because I know you have overcome. The future is bright, and eternity is not far off.

What does peace look like for you?

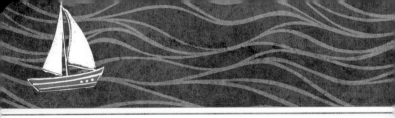

Perseverance

Do you not know that in a race all the runners run,
but only one gets the prize?
Run in such a way as to get the prize.

1 CORINTHIANS 9:24 NIV

I have tried hard to find you—
don't let me wander from your commands.

PSALM 119:10 NLT

I have fought the good fight,
I have finished the race,
I have kept the faith.

2 TIMOTHY 4:7 NCV

Let us not become weary in doing good, for at the proper
time we will reap a harvest if we do not give up.

GALATIANS 6:9 NIV

Lord, you are asking me to do something that is totally outside of my comfort zone. In fact, it edges on downright scary because of the strength it will take. Not only that, but it is incredibly time intensive. I can't do this, but you can. So, I surrender myself to your will. Please fill this empty vessel and have your way with me. As I pray these words, I can feel your power rising in me and a new, solid commitment to serve you regardless of the cost. This life is short, and I want to spend it doing whatever it takes to bring glory to your name and people into your kingdom.

What do you feel God is calling you to persevere in right now?

Praise

Sing to the Lord a new song,
his praise from the ends of the earth,
you who go down to the sea, and all that is in it,
you islands, and all who live in them.

Isaiah 42:10 NIV

Praise the LORD from the skies.
Praise him high above the earth.
Praise him, all you angels.
Praise him, all you armies of heaven.
Praise him, sun and moon.
Praise him, all you shining stars.
Praise him, highest heavens
and you waters above the sky.
Let them praise the LORD,
because they were created by his command.

Psalm 148:1-5 NCV

Precious Savior, where do I even begin? There are not enough hours in life to give you the praise you deserve. My heart swells and I cannot hold back. I praise you for your love, your salvation, your goodness, your faithfulness, your holiness, your righteousness, and your promises. I thank you that you are always with me, always for me, always working on my behalf. I am grateful for your blessings, your mercy, and your grace. I worship you for you are the great and almighty God, my king, my abba and the one I will praise forever—for now and in eternity.

What is something specific you can praise God for today?

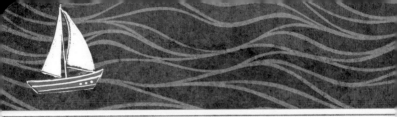

Prayer

At each and every sunrise you will hear my voice
as I prepare my sacrifice of prayer to you.
Every morning I lay out the pieces of my life on the altar
and wait for your fire to fall upon my heart.

PSALM 5:3 TPT

Make your life a prayer.

1 THESSALONIANS 5:17 TPT

The LORD does not listen to the wicked,
but he hears the prayers of those who do right.

PROVERBS 15:29 NCV

When you pray, go away by yourself, shut the door behind
you, and pray to your Father in private. Then your Father,
who sees everything, will reward you.

MATTHEW 6:6 NLT

Father, thank you that your door is always open, and your ears are attentive to my cry. Nothing is too big or too small to bring before your throne, for you care about every word I speak. I praise you for all that you are, my great and faithful God. I pray for my loved ones who know you to grow in you. I pray for those who don't know you to come to you. I pray for those who are hungry, homeless, and hurting that you would draw close and provide for them. I ask that you move me to be your hands and feet and use me to fulfill these requests I am asking of you.

What can you pray about right now?

Protection

My God is my rock. I can run to him for safety.
He is my shield and my saving strength,
my defender and my place of safety.
The LORD saves me from those who want to harm me.

2 SAMUEL 22:3 NCV

The LORD keeps you from all harm
and watches over your life.
The LORD keeps watch over you as you come and go,
both now and forever.

PSALM 121:7-8 NLT

The LORD is good, a refuge in times of trouble.
He cares for those who trust in him.

NAHUM 1:7 NIV

Father, this is hard, and it hurts. I didn't see it coming and now that it has, I feel bitterness rising in my heart. I want to strike back, but my respect for you restrains me. How can I halt the comments in my mind that keep torturing me with thoughts of revenge? I will run to you, fall at your feet in prayer, and ask that you protect me from my sinful desires. Help me to see and respond to this situation with your wisdom, mercy, and love. I know that you want to fight my battles so I release them to you, and I will wait to see your goodness.

How hard is it for you to lay down your battle plan and let God be your protector?

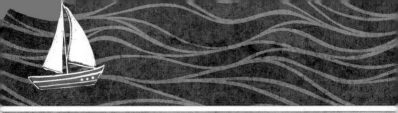

Provision

All scripture is inspired by God and is useful for
teaching, for reproof, for correction, and for training in
righteousness, so that everyone who belongs to God may
be proficient, equipped for every good work.

2 TIMOTHY 3:16–17 NRSV

May he give you the power to accomplish all the good
things your faith prompts you to do.

2 THESSALONIANS 1:11 NLT

We are God's handiwork, created in Christ Jesus to do
good works, which God prepared in advance for us to do.

EPHESIANS 2:10 NIV

"Seek the Kingdom of God above all else, and he will give
you everything you need. So don't be afraid, little flock.
For it gives your Father great happiness to give you the
Kingdom."

LUKE 12:31-32 NLT

Jehovah Jireh, my provider, your generosity exceeds any I could even begin to imagine. Not only have you given the solution to sin and offer of salvation, but you have also blessed me with abundant life here and everlasting life in heaven. I have everything I need in you to fulfill your will for me here on earth. With you, all things are possible. You are my greatest reward and I desire you more than breathe or life. Thank you for your power that is mightily working through me for your good pleasure. I praise you for your bountiful blessings.

How have you seen God provide for you lately?

Purpose

Christ's resurrection is your resurrection too. This is why we are to yearn for all that is above, for that's where Christ sits enthroned at the place of all power, honor, and authority.

<small>COLOSSIANS 3:1 TPT</small>

We know that in all things God works for the good of those who love him, who have been called according to his purpose.

<small>ROMANS 8:28 NIV</small>

My child, pay attention to my words; listen closely to what I say. Don't ever forget my words; keep them always in mind.

<small>PROVERBS 4:20-21 NCV</small>

It is God who works in you to will and to act in order to fulfill his good purpose.

<small>PHILIPPIANS 2:13 NIV</small>

Father, I confess that I have been going my own way lately. Life gets so hectic with repetitive household tasks, my job, and then the resulting exhaustion. In the depth of my heart, I want more than anything to live out your purpose for my life. I desire to seek you and your will for me, but it is hard to find time to do it. I must put you first, so today, I commit to pray, listen, and obey your direction. I don't want to miss a second of what you have planned for me. Fulfilling your purpose for my life will be my greatest priority.

How do you feel when you think about God having a special purpose for your life?

Reconciliation

We are made right with God by placing our faith in
Jesus Christ. And this is true for everyone who believes,
no matter who we are. For everyone has sinned; we
all fall short of God's glorious standard. Yet God, with
undeserved kindness, declares that we are righteous. He
did this through Christ Jesus when he freed us from the
penalty for our sins.

ROMANS 3:22–24 NLT

We have stopped evaluating others from a human point
of view. At one time we thought of Christ merely from
a human point of view. How differently we know him
now! This means that anyone who belongs to Christ has
become a new person. The old life is gone; a new life has
begun! And all of this is a gift from God, who brought us
back to himself through Christ. And God has given us
this task of reconciling people to him.

2 CORINTHIANS 5:16–18 NLT

Father, you know I care deeply about this person, but it seems as though there is no solution. It is painfully awkward to try and avoid the elephant in the room, yet neither of us have the courage to broach it. I know when I ignore resolution, I am evading your perfect will. You have called us to restoration and love, and by allowing this chasm to deepen, I am not at peace. I humble myself before you. Help me to forgive. I desire to obey you and to repair what has been broken. Please open their heart and mine and make us tender toward one another.

Can you believe God for reconciliation in your relationships?

Refreshment

The law of the LORD is perfect,
refreshing the soul.
The statutes of the LORD are trustworthy,
making wise the simple.

PSALM 19:7 NIV

How priceless is your unfailing love, O God!
People take refuge in the shadow of your wings.
They feast on the abundance of your house;
you give them drink from your river of delights.
For with you is the fountain of life;
in your light we see light.

PSALM 36:7–9 NIV

A generous person will prosper;
whoever refreshes others will be refreshed.

PROVERBS 11: 25 NIV

Lord, I must confess that I often seek the wrong type of recreation to restore my weary soul. I find myself in front of a screen watching things that are of no value and will even cause my thoughts to be unaligned with yours. I know that if I retreat with you to read your Word, listen to worship music, and pray, I will feel like I have rested fully. I will be renewed in mind, heart, and soul, and my life will reflect the fact that I have been in your presence. Help me come to you first for renewal, for only with you will I truly find rest and refreshment.

In what ways do you feel refreshed by God?

Relaxation

Blessed is the one who trusts in the LORD,
whose confidence is in him.
They will be like a tree planted by the water
that sends out its roots by the stream.
It does not fear when heat comes;
its leaves are always green.
It has no worries in a year of drought
and never fails to bear fruit.

JEREMIAH 17:7–8 NIV

"Those who love me, I will deliver;
I will protect those who know my name.
When they call to me, I will answer them;
I will be with them in trouble,
I will rescue them and honor them."

PSALM 91:14-15 NRSV

Lord, I can feel the warming peace of your abiding presence. You are always with me; it is me who fails to notice. You beckon me to sit at your feet as mine turn to run in a direction of busyness and tiresome errands. If only I would stop and put my activities on pause so I could linger with you, listening for your voice and hearing your answers for all that my life is asking of me. I will choose to come to a full stop and allow you to soothe my mind and calm my heart. I rejoice for I know I will find the relief and restoration I need in you.

How can you practice
relaxing in God's presence?

Reliability

The grass dries and withers and the flowers fall off,
but the Word of the Lord endures forever!

1 PETER 1:24-25 TPT

Every good action and every perfect gift is from God. These
good gifts come down from the Creator of the sun, moon,
and stars, who does not change like their shifting shadows.

JAMES 1:17 NCV

He will give eternal life to those who keep on doing good,
seeking after the glory and honor and immortality that
God offers.

ROMANS 2:7 NLT

You are near, LORD,
and all your commands are true.
Long ago I learned from your statutes
that you established them to last forever.

PSALM 119:151-152 NIV

*Father, from the newspaper to online to the radio, it is
exceedingly difficult to know who I can trust. It appears
there are so many competing statements and reports that
claim to be fact. Please give me your wisdom, discernment,
and revelation to comprehend what is truth and what isn't.
I am so thankful that amidst the noise and confusion you
are trustworthy, and I can always count on the accuracy of
the Bible. It is my guide for life, your living breathing Word to
direct me here and someday safely home to you.*

How does it make you feel knowing you can rely on God for everything?

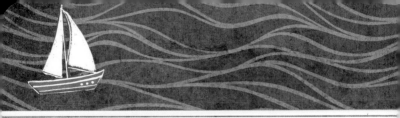

Relief

"I am the Alpha and the Omega—the Beginning and the
End. To all who are thirsty I will give freely from the
springs of the water of life."

REVELATION 21:6 NLT

I prayed to the LORD, and he answered me.
He freed me from all my fears.
Those who look to him for help will be radiant with joy.

PSALM 34:4–5 NLT

The Spirit helps us in our weakness. We do not know
what we ought to pray for, but the Spirit himself
intercedes for us through wordless groans. And he
who searches our hearts knows the mind of the Spirit,
because the Spirit intercedes for God's people in
accordance with the will of God.

ROMANS 8:26–27 NIV

Jesus, if not for you I would be completely overwhelmed by this life. My comfort is in knowing that regardless of what I face here, you have overcome the world. When I feel weak, I only need to trust in your strength to carry me through. Your living water revives me, quenching my spiritual thirst. When I call, you answer in your perfect knowledge. Holy Spirit, please pray for me in ways I can't, interceding for me and asking God in his wisdom to give me only what I need at this very moment.

What relief do you need from God in your current situation?

Restoration

He has saved us and called us to a holy life—not because of anything we have done but because of his own purpose and grace.

2 TIMOTHY 1:9 NIV

"Let us praise the Lord, the God of Israel,
because he has come to help his people and has given them freedom.
He has given us a powerful Savior."

LUKE 1:68-69 NCV

We can boldly enter heaven's Most Holy Place because of the blood of Jesus. By his death, Jesus opened a new and life-giving way through the curtain into the Most Holy Place. And since we have a great High Priest who rules over God's house, let us go right into the presence of God with sincere hearts fully trusting him.

HEBREWS 10:19—22 NLT

God, without you I know what a mess I would be. I have lived for a time without you, and it was miserable. I am so thankful that because of the work your Son did on the cross, you now look at me and see a righteous person. I can live a holy life because you have empowered me through your Spirit. I have access to bring my prayers before your throne because Jesus tore the veil. I am saved, I am sealed, and I am a child of the King. I praise you for your gift of grace that has given me a life of freedom in Christ.

How have you experienced the power of restoration in your life?

Reward

Work willingly at whatever you do, as though you were
working for the Lord rather than for people. Remember
that the Lord will give you an inheritance as your reward,
and that the Master you are serving is Christ.

COLOSSIANS 3:23-24 NLT

"Love your enemies, do good to them, and lend to them
without expecting to get anything back. Then your
reward will be great, and you will be children of the Most
High, because he is kind to the ungrateful and wicked."

LUKE 6:35 NIV

Without faith living within us it would be impossible to
please God. For we come to God in faith knowing that
he is real and that he rewards the faith of those who
passionately seek him.

HEBREWS 11:6 TPT

Father, isn't it enough that you love me so deeply and have given me salvation and eternal life? You want to reward me as well? It is a joy and a privilege to seek you, do good to others, and even to suffer for your name. Believing that you exist? There is evidence everywhere! I praise you God most high that your existence is evident in the blue sky, a baby's cry, and the love of a friend. Help me serve you and others, doing it with consistency and a heart filled with gratitude for your goodness. You, Lord, are my reward.

How does it make you feel knowing that God will reward you for your diligence?

Safety

The LORD also will be a refuge for the oppressed,
A refuge in times of trouble.
Those who know Your name will put their trust in You;
For You, LORD, have not forsaken those who seek You.

PSALM 9:9–10 NKJV

I call to you from the ends of the earth when I am afraid.
Carry me away to a high mountain.
You have been my protection,
like a strong tower against my enemies.

PSALM 61:2-3 NCV

"Don't be afraid of anyone,
because I am with you to protect you," says the LORD.

JEREMIAH 1:8 NCV

Dear Father, I am so thankful that you have promised to never leave me or forsake me. You see every pothole before I fall in it, and you have paved my way. You take problems that I have made mountains of and easily diminish them with your wisdom. I praise you for the comfort I receive as you hide me under your wings, pulling me close so you can protect me. You are my great defender who takes my distress and extinguishes it. I praise you, for with you I am triumphant. Thank you for being my helper and my hope.

Do you feel safe when you think about God being near you?

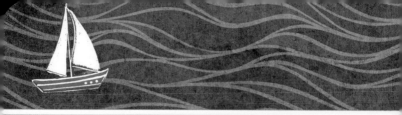

Salvation

"This is how God loved the world: He gave his one and only Son, so that everyone who believes in him will not perish but have eternal life."

JOHN 3:16 NLT

The wages of sin is death,
but the gift of God is eternal life in Christ Jesus our Lord.

ROMANS 6:23 NIV

By grace you have been saved by faith. Nothing you did could ever earn this salvation, for it was the love gift from God that brought us to Christ!

EPHESIANS 2:8 TPT

If you openly declare that Jesus is Lord and believe in your heart that God raised him from the dead, you will be saved.

ROMANS 10:9 NLT

Jesus, I am dumbfounded when I encounter people who reject your gift of salvation. You left heaven to come and humble yourself to death on a cross for sin you never committed. Many I have shared the gospel with say it's too easy just to expect to be forgiven. It wasn't easy for you. I shudder at your suffering, yet I thank you for your broken body and poured out blood that has saved me from sin, death, and eternal separation from God. Help me to be bold about sharing your salvation so many can come to know the greatest sacrifice and love of all.

How do you respond to the message of salvation?

Strength

God is our refuge and strength,
an ever-present help in trouble.

Psalm 46:1-3 NIV

The Lord is faithful, and he will strengthen you
and protect you from the evil one.

2 Thessalonians 3:3 NIV

"Don't be afraid, for I am with you.
Don't be discouraged, for I am your God.
I will strengthen you and help you.
I will hold you up with my victorious right hand."

Isaiah 41:10 NLT

Lord, don't be far away.
You are my strength; hurry to help me.

Psalm 22:19 NCV

Father, your Word warns me to be aware of my enemy. He is sly and often worms his way in with the most subtle of tactics. I have found myself believing his lies again, and I am here to confess. I am so thankful that I can pick up your Word that reminds me you are far greater and have already won the victory. Help me stay consistent in studying your Scripture, arming myself with your truth for all spiritual battles. I praise you for your faithfulness in always showing up strong on my behalf. Thank you for providing a way out for me as I trust in and follow you.

What makes you feel strong?

Stress

Praise the LORD, my soul;
all my inmost being, praise his holy name.
Praise the LORD, my soul,
and forget not all his benefits—
who forgives all your sins and heals all your diseases,
who redeems your life from the pit
and crowns you with love and compassion,
who satisfies your desires with good things
so that your youth is renewed like the eagle's.

PSALM 103:1-5 NIV

Commit your actions to the LORD.
and your plans will succeed.

PROVERBS 16:3 NLT

As pressure and stress bear down on me,
I find joy in your commands.

PSALM 119:143 NLT

Lord, I really do mean to have consistent time with you each day. Then the day takes on a life of its own and tends to run me more than I run it. I do hear your Spirit whisper priorities, and mine are most definitely off. My hectic schedule brings stress but sitting in your presence promotes peace. I can't handle the daily demands without you. With you I find wisdom, instruction, and guidance that will address and help me navigate anything the day throws at me. I commit myself to you, Lord, and ask that you help me meet you every day.

When was the last time you were able to let go of stress and just sit with God?

Support

Whom have I in heaven but you?
And earth has nothing I desire besides you.
My flesh and my heart may fail,
but God is the strength of my heart
and my portion forever.

PSALM 73:25–26 NIV

You, God, see the trouble of the afflicted;
you consider their grief and take it in hand.
The victims commit themselves to you;
you are the helper of the fatherless.

PSALM 10:14 NIV

You are my hiding place;
You shall preserve me from trouble;
You shall surround me with songs of deliverance.

PSALM 32:7 NKJV

Lord, I can't find the words to talk about this issue. You are the only one I can run to who knows how I feel and how I am hurting without me saying anything. I don't want to share my sorrow with anyone right now, but I find comfort in knowing you understand it completely without a spoken syllable. Thank you for your deep compassion that moves you to keep my tears. As I weep, I can sense your presence wrapping around me like a warm blanket. Just knowing how near you are starts to lift my spirit and helps me believe that I will smile again soon.

When do you feel the most supported by God?

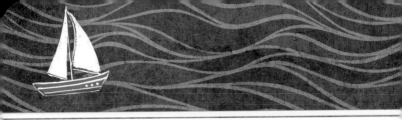

Sustenance

God is able to bless you abundantly,
so that in all things at all times, having all that you need,
you will abound in every good work.

2 CORINTHIANS 9:8 NIV

I fall to my knees and pray to the Father, the Creator of
everything in heaven and on earth. I pray that from his
glorious, unlimited resources he will empower you with
inner strength through his Spirit. Then Christ will make
his home in your hearts as you trust in him. Your roots
will grow down into God's love and keep you strong.
And may you have the power to understand, as all God's
people should, how wide, how long, how high, and how
deep his love is. May you experience the love of Christ,
though it is too great to understand fully. Then you will
be made complete with all the fullness of life and power
that comes from God.

EPHESIANS 3:14–19 NLT

Lord, this world has so many things, so many pastimes that grab my attention and desire my time. When I have indulged in some, although harmless, they leave me feeling empty and wanting my wasted hours back. You, on the other hand, offer me every good and worthy thing. At your feet, I become strong; I learn love and I gain understanding. Help me choose the things that lead to deeper knowledge of you. I pray I will run to your Word to be restored. I ask that you help me to choose time spent with you over meaningless activities. Help me seek you first.

How do you get your sustenance from God?

Trust

Those who know the LORD trust him,
because he will not leave those who come to him.

PSALM 9:10 NCV

I trust in you, LORD. I say, "You are my God."
My whole life is in your hands.
Save me from the hands of my enemies.
Save me from those who are chasing me.

PSALM 31:14-15 NIV

Yes, the LORD is for me; he will help me.
I will look in triumph at those who hate me.
It is better to take refuge in the LORD
than to trust in people.

PSALM 118:7-8 NLT

Lord, I want to thank you all the times you have heard my prayers. You have never failed to answer me although sometimes it was not as I had hoped. In your wisdom, you know things that I don't, and your no is because you have all the knowledge and understanding needed to work for my best interest. In my heart, I desire to become more like you and only you know what that journey requires. I commit myself to you in faith, for I know that I can always trust you to protect and guide me on the path you have designed for me.

How do you know that God is trustworthy?

Victory

The horse is made ready for the day of battle,
But the victory rests with the LORD.

PROVERBS 21:31 NIV

Every child of God defeats this evil world,
and we achieve this victory through our faith.

1 JOHN 5:4 NLT

Say to the anxious and fearful,
"Be strong and never afraid.
Look, here comes your God!
He is breaking through to give you victory!
He comes to avenge your enemies.
With divine retribution he comes to save you!"

ISAIAH 35:4 TPT

"The LORD your God is the one who goes with you to fight
for you against your enemies to give you victory."

DEUTERONOMY 20:4 NIV

Father, like the child on the playground that brags about their daddy to the other kids, I want to boast about you. You, Abba, are almighty, stronger than any other, and able to do all things because for you the miraculous is effortless. You love me like no one else, and if I were in trouble, you would part the seas and open the skies to come to my defense. This is how I see you and why I praise you. There is none like you; you are my everything and I am amazed at how you care for me. Thank you for always being my hero, the lover of my soul, and the one who will always reign victorious.

You win with Jesus in your life! Can you think of the last victory you experienced?

Wholeness

For you who fear my name,
the sun of righteousness shall rise
with healing in its wings.

MALACHI 4:2 ESV

Celebrate with praises the God and Father of our Lord
Jesus Christ, who has shown us his extravagant mercy.
For his fountain of mercy has given us a new life—we are
reborn to experience a living, energetic hope through
the resurrection of Jesus Christ from the dead. We are
reborn into a perfect inheritance that can never perish,
never be defiled, and never diminish. It is promised
and preserved forever in the heavenly realm for you!
Through our faith, the mighty power of God constantly
guards us until our full salvation is ready to be revealed
in the last time.

1 PETER 1:3–5 TPT

Father, as I try to squeeze into something that will never fit, I become frustrated with my inability to have self-control. I have prayed repeatedly for restraint with my temptations, yet I place the thing that makes me fall within my reach. I am so grateful that you show me grace. I read your Word and am inspired to surrender my shortcomings to you, for you will give me the strength needed to overcome. In faith, I receive your power to triumph over this temporary physical state and look forward to the day when all you have in store for me is revealed.

How does understanding eternal wholeness benefit you in this life?

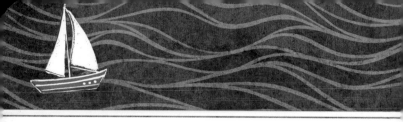

Wisdom

Wisdom will come into your mind,
and knowledge will be pleasing to you.
Good sense will protect you;
understanding will guard you
It will keep you from the wicked,
from those whose words are bad.

PROVERBS 2:10-12 NCV

Wisdom and money can get you almost anything,
but only wisdom can save your life.

ECCLESIASTES 7:12 NLT

If any of you lacks wisdom, you should ask God,
who gives generously to all without finding fault,
and it will be given to you.

JAMES 1:5 NIV

Lord, I had a chance today to say something nice, to encourage someone, and instead I picked a fight. I know what I should do, but I end up doing the exact opposite. I feel terrible, and I have damaged a relationship that I cherish all because I wanted to be right. In every way, I was wrong. Please forgive me and help me to turn from my foolish ways. I ask for wisdom, believing you will give it to me as your Word says. Help understanding and prudence instruct the motive of my heart. Lead me to think before I speak and put others' needs and feelings above my own.

How can you use God's wisdom to make better choices?

Worry

Leave all your cares and anxieties at the feet of the Lord,
and measureless grace will strengthen you.

PSALM 55:22 TPT

"Who of you by worrying
can add a single hour to your life?"

LUKE 12:25 NIV

Worry weighs a person down;
an encouraging word cheers a person up.

PROVERBS 12:25 NLT

Do not worry about anything, but pray and ask God for
everything you need, always giving thanks. And God's
peace, which is so great we cannot understand it, will
keep your hearts and minds in Christ Jesus.

PHILIPPIANS 4:6-7 NCV

Lord, I feel anxiety taking over, creating those out-of-control jitters inside my stomach. This is unhealthy and not what you want for me. Your Word says I have no reason to fear, and it's like throwing valuable hours in the trash if I spend them fretting. Worry robs my joy and chases friends away as I drone on about my troubles. So instead, I will trust you, and I will pray in faith believing you have mastered it all. I receive your peace, knowing you can do all things. Assurance of your power fills me. I can face whatever comes fearlessly, for you alone are my salvation.

What worries can you hand over to God today?

BroadStreet Publishing Group, LLC.
Savage, Minnesota USA
Broadstreetpublishing.com

PRAYERS & PROMISES FOR DAILY STRENGTH

9781424565795 (faux)
9781424564637 (softcover)
9781424565207 (eBook)

Prayers composed by Suzanne Niles.

Design and typesetting by Garborg Design Works | garborgdesign.com
Compiled and edited by Michelle Winger | literallyprecise.com

Printed in the United States of America.

23 24 25 26 27 28 29   7 6 5 4 3 2 1

Lord, I feel anxiety taking over, creating those out-of-control jitters inside my stomach. This is unhealthy and not what you want for me. Your Word says I have no reason to fear, and it's like throwing valuable hours in the trash if I spend them fretting. Worry robs my joy and chases friends away as I drone on about my troubles. So instead, I will trust you, and I will pray in faith believing you have mastered it all. I receive your peace, knowing you can do all things. Assurance of your power fills me. I can face whatever comes fearlessly, for you alone are my salvation.

What worries can you hand over to God today?

BroadStreet Publishing Group, LLC.
Savage, Minnesota USA
Broadstreetpublishing.com

PRAYERS & PROMISES FOR DAILY STRENGTH
© 2022 by BroadStreet Publishing

9781424565795 (faux)
9781424564637 (softcover)
9781424565207 (eBook)

Prayers composed by Suzanne Niles.

Design and typesetting by Garborg Design Works | garborgdesign.com
Compiled and edited by Michelle Winger | literallyprecise.com

Printed in the United States of America.

23 24 25 26 27 28 29   7 6 5 4 3 2 1

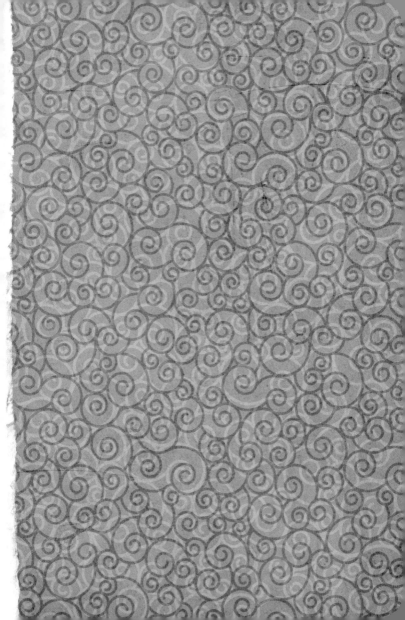

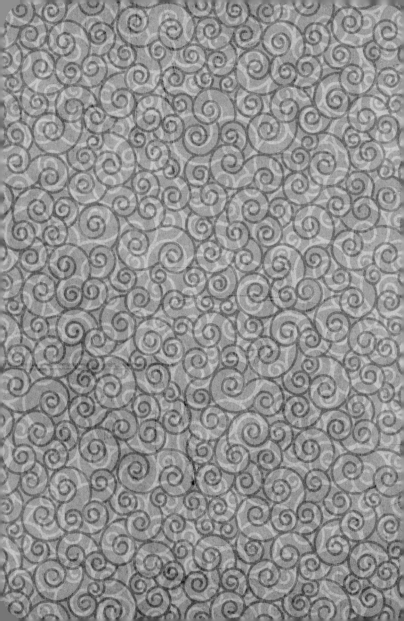